Contents

Introduction	4
Here, There And Everywhere	6
Back In The U.S.S.R.	11
And Your Bird Can Sing	19
Don't Let Me Down	26
Dear Prudence	32
Get Back	40
Lucy In The Sky With Diamonds	48
Sgt. Pepper's Lonely Hearts Club Band	54
Reading Tablature	62

Introduction

Here are a few pointers to get the best from this book... and the DVD too.

Using the DVD

Time Code

Every tutorial and song layout contains several timings in these boxes. They'll tell you whereabouts on the relevant video you'll find more info, a play-through or other example.

On the DVD, you'll find a full tutorial video for every song that's in the book. Each video looks at the most important features of the song, including all the chord shapes and some essential techniques—such as strumming or picking patterns—before playing each section of the song through. Finally there's a run-though of the entire song using professionally produced backing tracks.

Watch out for the time code symbols in the book (*left*). Whenever you see this, you'll know what section of the video to watch for more info or to hear an example. The time shown is the time of the particular track on the DVD.

Reading Repeats

Repeat Marks

Music between these two symbols is repeated. Go back to the first symbol and play again from there.

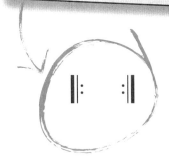

In written music, repeated sections are often used to show a section that's played more than once. Repeats might be immediate (verse 2 following directly on from verse 1, for example) or they might be a return to a passage from earlier on in the song. There are specific ways to show both kinds of repeats.

The simplest kind of repeat is one between the two repeat marks (*left*). These *repeat marks* embrace a passage to be repeated.

Simply play the section through and, when you finish it, play it again from the start of the section.

Repeat Endings

The square brackets above the music show different endings for the first and second time through a repeated section: the endings are numbered.

Repeated sections like this often have different endings on the first and second play through. These are shown by square brackets over the endings, known as *first* and *second time* bars. Sometimes you'll even see third or fourth time bars.

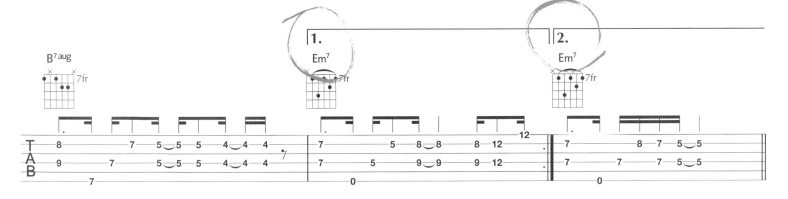

PLAY it RIGHT
THE BEATLES 1966–1969
LEARN 8 CLASSIC BEATLES SONGS ON GUITAR
DAVID HARRISON

Wise Publications
part of The Music Sales Group
London/New York/Paris/Sydney/Copenhagen/Berlin/Madrid/Hong Kong/Tokyo

Published by
Wise Publications
14-15 Berners Street,
London W1T 3LJ, UK.

Exclusive Distributors:
Music Sales Limited
Distribution Centre, Newmarket Road,
Bury St Edmunds, Suffolk IP33 3YB, UK.
Music Sales Corporation
180 Madison Avenue, 24th Floor,
New York NY 10016, USA.
Music Sales Pty Limited
Units 3-4, 17 Willfox Street, Condell Park
NSW 2200, Australia.

Order No. AM1005378
ISBN 978-1-78038-714-7

This book © Copyright 2013 Wise Publications,
a division of Music Sales Limited.

Unauthorised reproduction of any part of this
publication by any means including photocopying is an
infringement of copyright.

Edited by Toby Knowles.
Music processing and layout by Shedwork.

Printed in the EU.

More Repeats: Segno and Coda

Another common type of repeat occurs when the music returns to a section played earlier in the song. This is often followed by a jump to the ending.

Look out for this symbol 𝄋, called a *segno*. This shows where to return to. You'll be sent there by an instruction at the end of a section: *D. S.* which stands for *dal segno* ('from the sign').

Generally, when you're playing from the 𝄋 you're headed towards the *coda*, the final section of the song. So watch out for the symbol. You'll see *To coda*, which is telling you to jump to the Coda section.

Dal Segno

Watch out for a D.S. at the end of a section. It sends you back to the 𝄋 symbol. This often leads to a coda.

Coda

The coda (meaning 'tail' in Italian) is the last section of a song. It's signalled with . It might include a final chorus or outro. Look for the 'To coda' instruction.

Where you're sent to the 𝄋 first, you'll see 'D.S. al Coda' meaning 'from the sign, to the coda'.

Chord Boxes

The vertical lines represent the guitar strings from the bottom string (left) to the top string (right).

The horizontal lines are the fret wires, and the nut is shown as a thick line at the top.

Open strings are shown with 'o', strings not played with 'x'.

Fret numbers are shown when the nut is out of view.

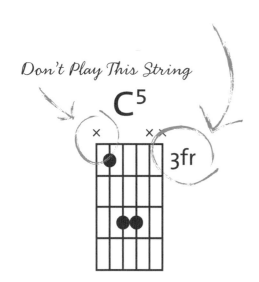

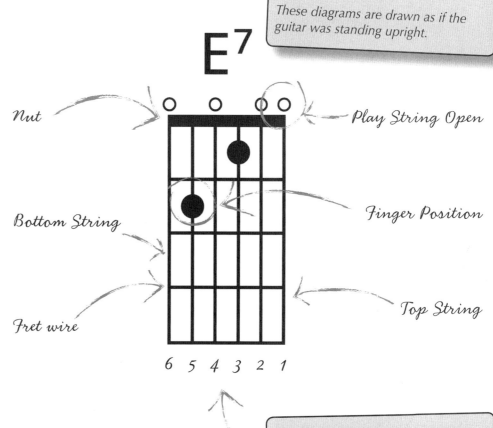

Which Way Up?

These diagrams are drawn as if the guitar was standing upright.

String Numbers

Strings are numbered from top (1st) to bottom (6th).

Here, There And Everywhere

This McCartney composition was written for the 1966 album Revolver. It features a famous key signature change between the verse and bridge.

Playing the Intro

The song begins with five chords, each strummed once through. Strum them slowly, so that you can almost hear each string individually. This will create a more dramatic feel that makes a feature of the unaccompanied guitar in this section.

To lead a better life, I need my love to be here.

Verse Strumming

The verse can either be strummed or picked. If you choose to strum, try a loose pattern like the one shown here.

Move the strumming hand down and up in continuous sixteenths, even when you're not making contact with the strings.

This will create a more even and relaxed rhythm, and means you can add extra sixteenths at any point if you like.

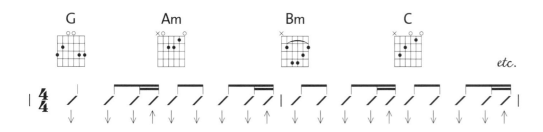

Verse Picking

Each chord in the verse lasts for two beats, and the pattern is designed to bring out the main features of each chord in the time available.

Pick the bass note with the thumb—it'll be on the 6th, 5th or 4th string—and then half a beat later pick the next string up.

On the second beat add some upper notes together picked on two or three strings, depending how many you have spare and the effect you're after.

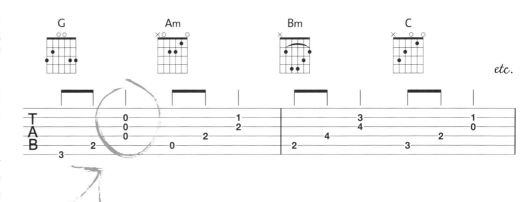

On G, for example, you might choose to play the 4th, 3rd and 2nd strings together. On Am, where the bass note is on the 5th string, you might only add two extra strings to the chord.

There's no hard and fast rule about this, so experiment until the pattern is smooth and consistent, adding or omitting notes from the chord as you like. Introducing slight accents will also create interest.

Bridge

`03:37`

There's a momentary but dramatic change of key at this point, from G major to B♭ major. Continue with the same picking pattern for the four-bar bridge. In the third bar, a single chord lasts for four beats, so you'll need to repeat the pattern (or fill in with a variation like the one shown here). In the song tab, the picking pattern isn't written out for the individual chords, but here it is in full.

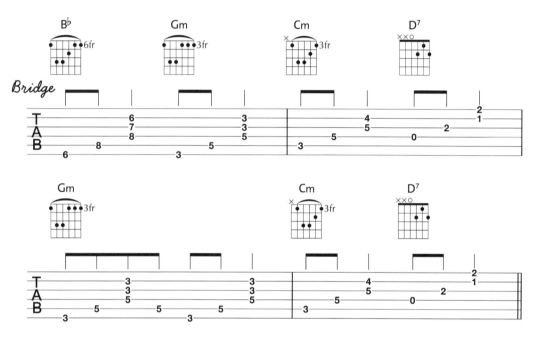

Bridge Lead Line

`04:24`

In the final two bars of the bridge, there's an alternative guitar part: a little lead line to take us back into the verse.

It ends on a pair of strings picked slightly apart.

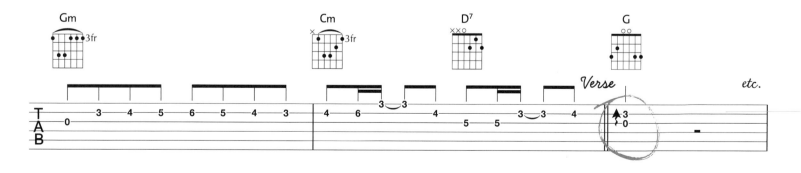

Back In The U.S.S.R.

This iconic 1968 track by McCartney that opens The White Album *clearly shows the Chuck Berry influence in its famous guitar riff—and there's a nod to The Beach Boys in the bridge section, too.*

Intro

The song opens with a short intro section on E⁷. The lead guitar plays a little detail followed by a couple of stabs on the top two strings—both strings playing the same E note (*right*).

The rhythm guitar plays eighth-notes on the E⁷ chord, building in volume throughout the intro: this gives a real lift to the following chorus section.

Start by strumming softly on just the bottom couple of strings, extending the strum to include higher strings as your strum becomes heavier (*below*).

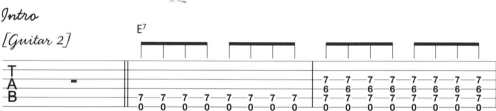

Changing Tone

Start by muting lightly with the strumming hand, gradually releasing the mute until the strings are free to ring out. This will create a gradual increase in volume and sustain.

Verse

The Chuck Berry-style rhythmic riff that's played throughout the verse is based on simple two-note shapes moving to different positions on the fingerboard.

- Firstly A⁵ and A⁶ on the 5th fret:

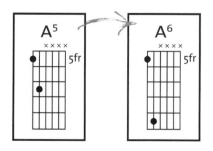

- Then the same thing up on the 10th fret, playing D⁵ and D⁶:

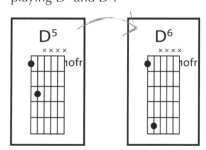

- And finally two frets lower, on the 10th fret, for C⁵ and C⁶:

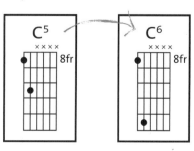

The entire verse is 8 bars long—in fact, it's just a repeated 4-bar sequence.

Keep the picking fingers (or plectrum) very tight to the strings to create the crisp, precise rhythm we're after.

Strum down on the eighths, with a quick down-up for the sixteenths too. Here are the first four bars.

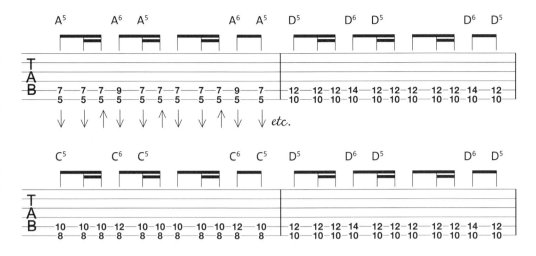

Two Guitar Parts

Play either the Guitar 1 (top line) or Guitar 3 (bottom line) part for the first 4 bars. In the final bar of the chorus, however, play all the notes with a single guitar.

 ## Chorus

The rhythmic riff played in the verse continues into the chorus, moving up and down the neck as the chords dictate: a bar each of A, C and D.

Two further lead guitars playing single note lines in octaves. After three bars there's a break, and two bars later the 1st guitar plays three pairs of notes in 6ths.

Walk-up

In the second chorus, the same octave line is played, but at the break another two bars of 3/4 are inserted and this time the chorus leads to a bridge by means of a four-note walk-up on the bottom string:

Playing the Walk-up

Be sure to play each note of this bass line evenly and crisply for the Beach Boys feel to be effective.

Bridge

The bridge is generally acknowledged to be a pastiche of the Beach Boys style so popular at the time this track was written, with soaring, falsetto backing and doo-wop bass vocals.

The guitar part is built on very deliberately strummed eighth-notes for eight bars: firstly pairs of strums on the first and third beats, and then constant down-strums on a descending sequence of chords.

For the song, this is all written out as strumming rhythms, but here it is in full tab.

Strumming the Bridge

Strum the constant eighths with down-strums to create a regular, even sound.

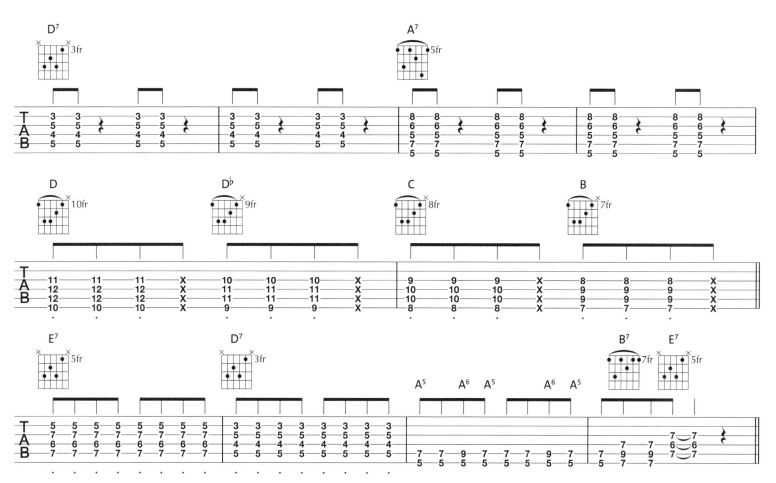

Outro

The song ends with the first bar of the octave line from the chorus played six times through, before a pair of notes an octave apart.

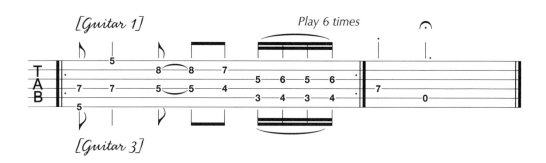

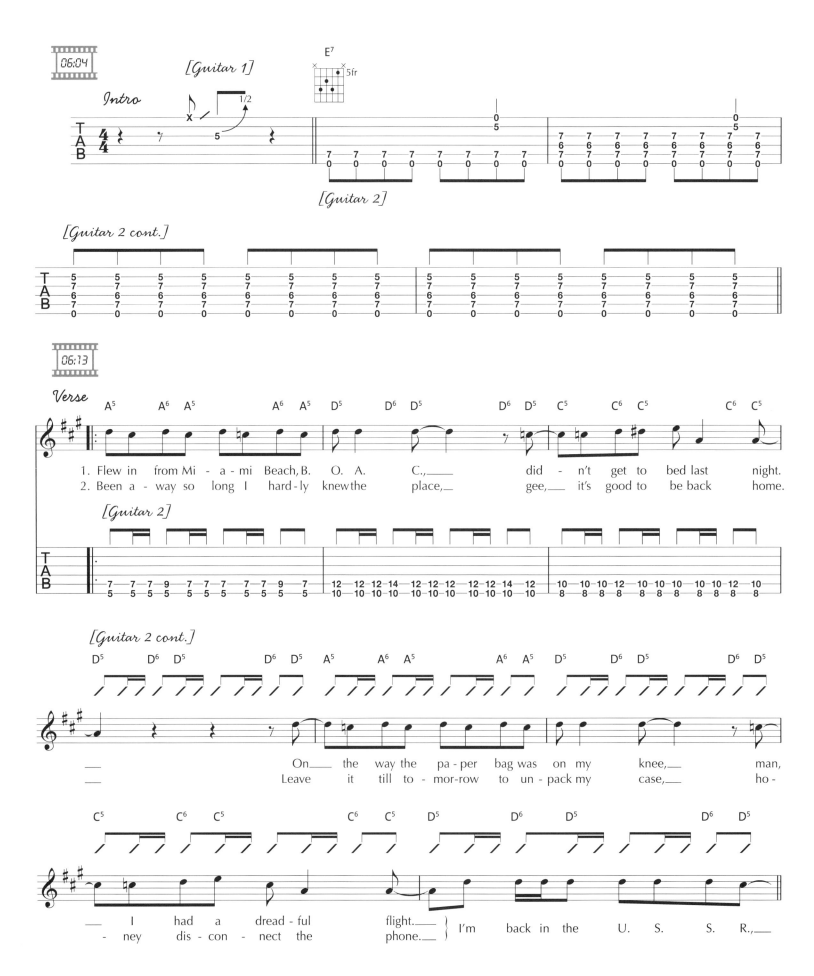

And Your Bird Can Sing

From the 1966 album Revolver, *this Lennon composition features various sections with an instrumental guitar duet, originally played by Paul McCartney and George Harrison.*

Playing the Intro

Recycling Guitar Parts

These parts reappear in extended form in the guitar solo and again in the outro, so although there's a fair bit to work on it'll be worth your while!

The two guitar parts that open the song are rhythmically identical, they both begin on the open 6th string but then harmonise a third—and at times a fourth—apart.

Both parts contain slides and bends, and are based on climbing and descending scale passages in the key of E major. Here's the guitar 1 part:

Intro [Guitar 1]

The guitar 2 part, lower than guitar 1, has a whole tone bend at the end of the third bar, where the guitar 1 part has a half-tone bend. The tuning here is crucial to avoid ugly clashes between the parts. Here's how the guitar 2 part looks:

Intro [Guitar 2]

Verse

In contrast, the verse consists of simple strumming in quarter-notes through an 8-bar section.

At the end of verse 1, the original contains the guitar parts from the final bar of the intro—minus the very first note of the bar.

Verse 1 Only

This detail doesn't appear in verse 2, which instead leads straight into the bridge section.

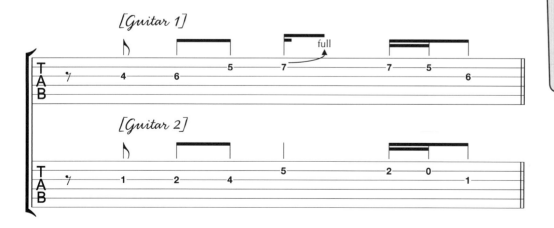

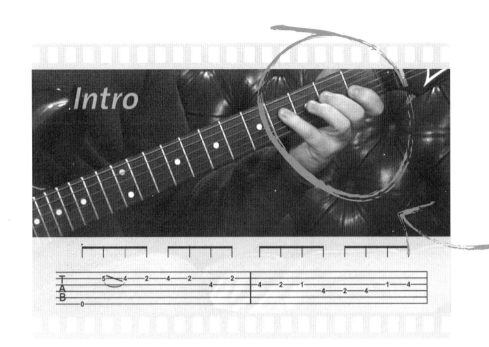

Sensible Fingering

It's important to make sure that your fretting fingers are under control: use your fourth finger to help with the stretches, and you'll find everything's easier to locate.

Bridge

Another guitar duet forms the basis of this 8-bar section. This time, rather than going up and down scales, the parts essentially climb up and down arpeggios of the chords. Guitar 1 reaches up to the top string in each bar:

[Guitar 1]

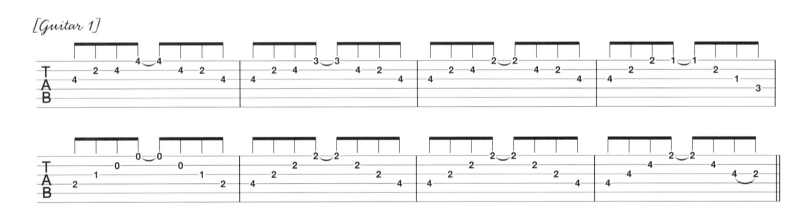

Guitar 2, meanwhile, plays a string lower throughout. The first three bars are the same as each other:

[Guitar 2]

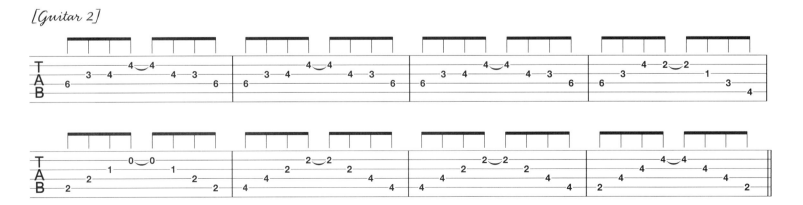

Guitar Solo

The guitar solo begins by playing the 4-bar intro in both guitar parts, and continues in a similar fashion. Here are the remaining four bars for the 1st guitar (*right*):

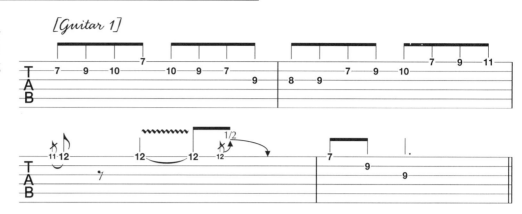

The guitar 2 part for the solo continues like this (*below*):

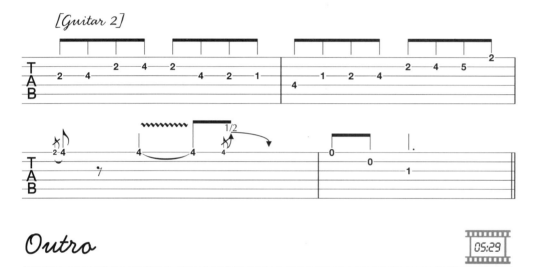

Outro

The outro is another run-through of the guitar solo in both guitar parts, before the first bar of the intro/solo is repeated three times over.

The song ends on a single A chord.

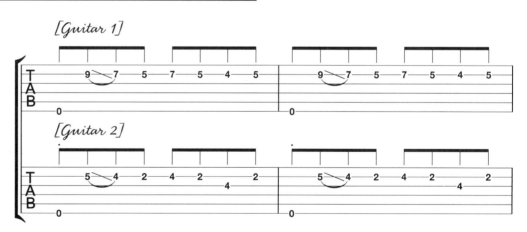

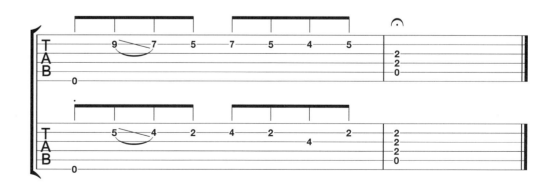

And Your Bird Can Sing
Words & Music by John Lennon & Paul McCartney

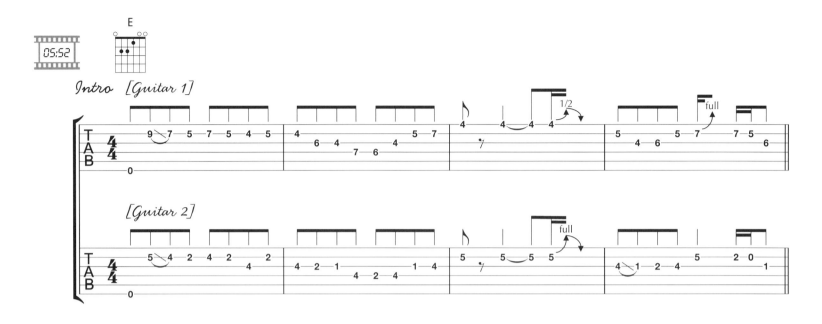

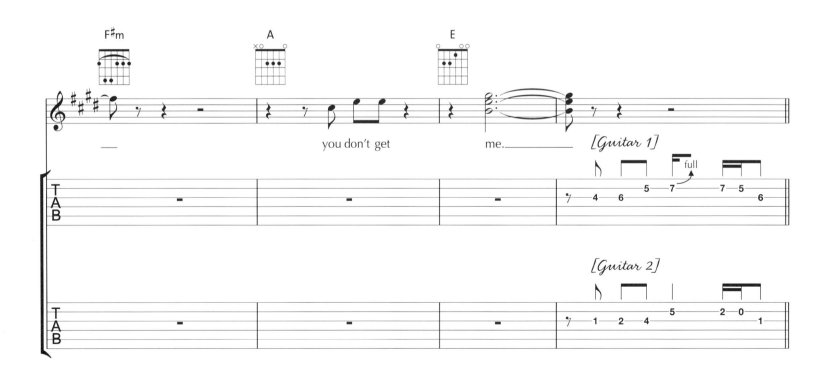

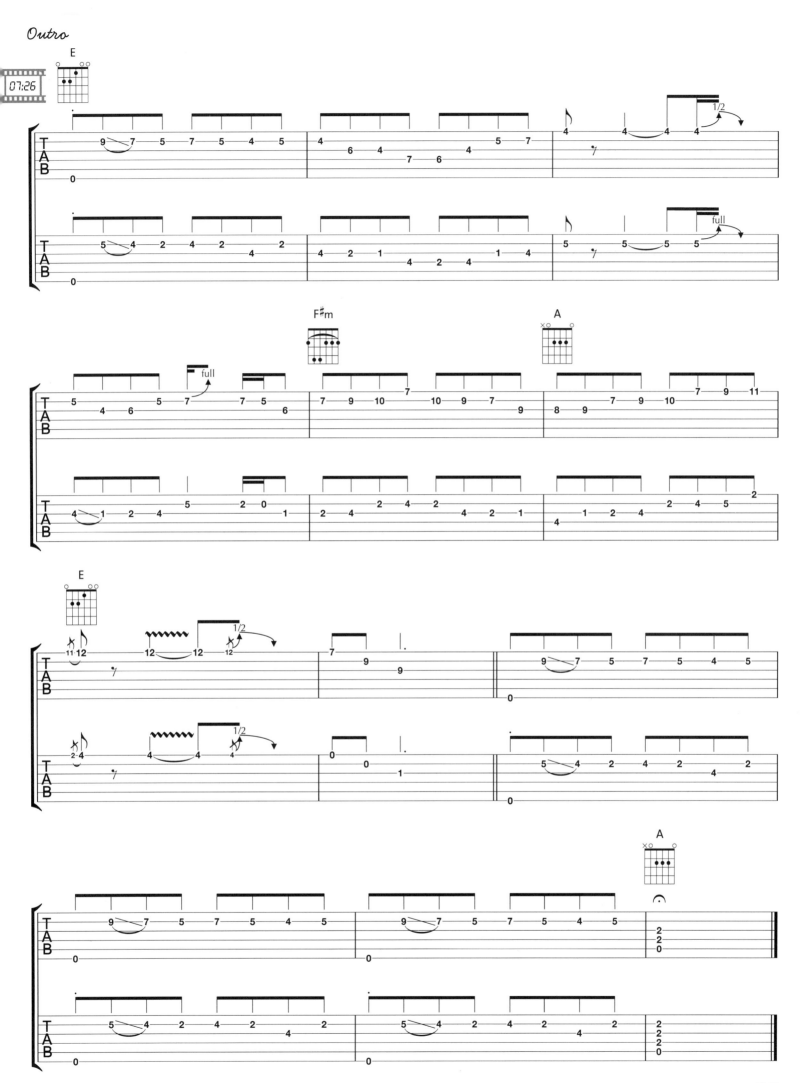

Don't Let Me Down

Hammer-on
Pick the first note, and bring the next finger smartly down onto the finger board without picking again. If you're firm and accurate the new note will sound clearly.

This plaintive love song by John Lennon was seen as a heartfelt plea to Yoko Ono. It's a very simple song, but with time signature changes and some intricate guitar parts there's plenty to play.

Intro Lick

⏱ 00:35

Intro

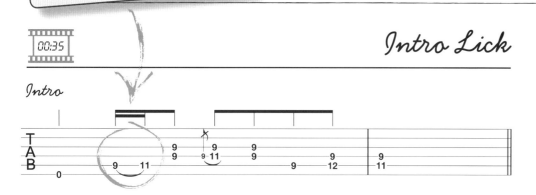

The phrase that kicks off the song reappears in various other places too.

Barre across the 3rd, 4th and 5th strings at the 9th fret, using the third and fourth fingers to play the notes on the 11th and 12th frets.

If you're careful to finger the notes correctly the phrase should pretty much fall into place.

Chorus

⏱ 01:42

The original main guitar part is a combination of strumming a specific rhythm on a higher F#m shape together with the lick we just looked at.

The final bar overlaps with the beginning of the verse, and has 5 beats on a held pair of notes. Be sure to count the extra beat when the time signature momentarily changes.

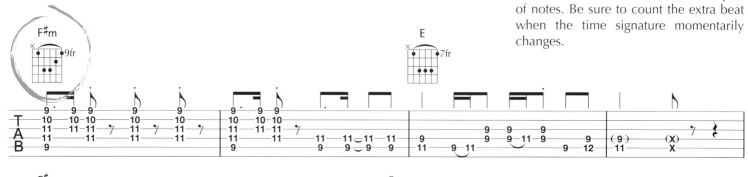

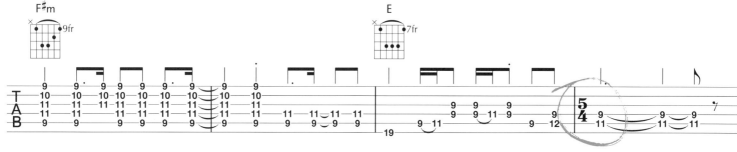

26

Verse Picking

The main guitar figure in the verse involves pairs of notes on adjacent strings and slides. Notice the 5/4 bar halfway through, too. You'll be able to keep your place quite easily if you count the beats out firmly to yourself—or sing the tune!

Picking Technique

To pick the notes, use a plectrum for the lower note, but the second or third finger to play the upper note.

Alternatively, do away with the plectrum altogether and pick the notes with the thumb and first finger.

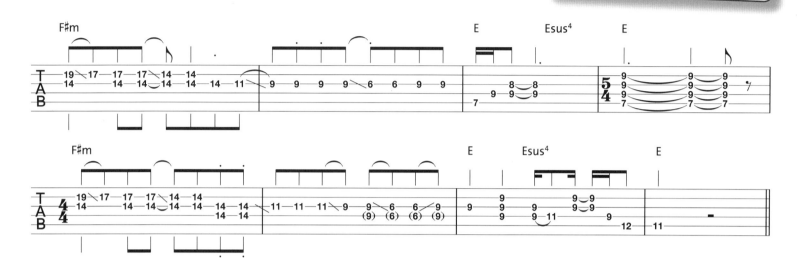

Bridge

The rhythm guitar strums the chords in a particular way: pick two eighths on the bottom note of the chord, followed by full strums in the rhythm shown.

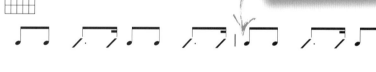

Picking Notation

Pick the bottom note of the chord only where you see round-headed notes.

Strumming Notation

Strum as normal where you see rhythm notation.

The lead guitar, meanwhile, plays a descending single-note line, ending on the familiar phrase from the intro.

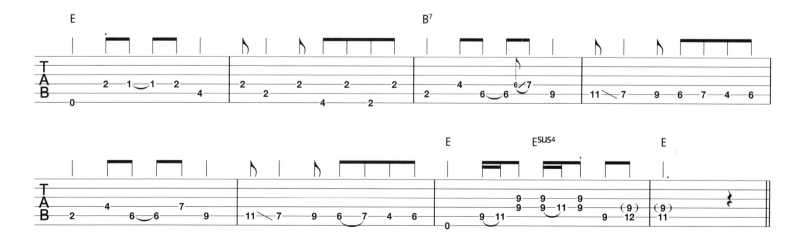

27

Don't Let Me Down
Words & Music by John Lennon & Paul McCartney

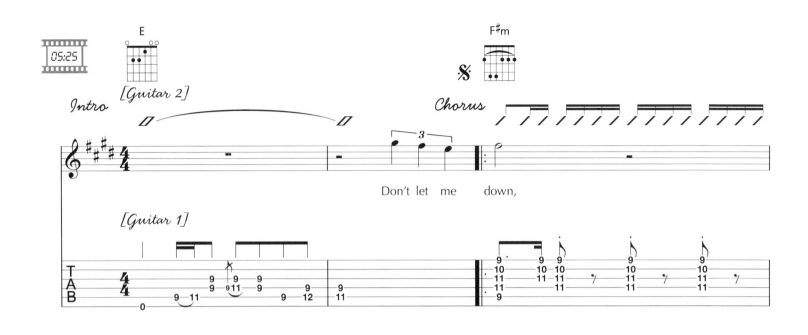
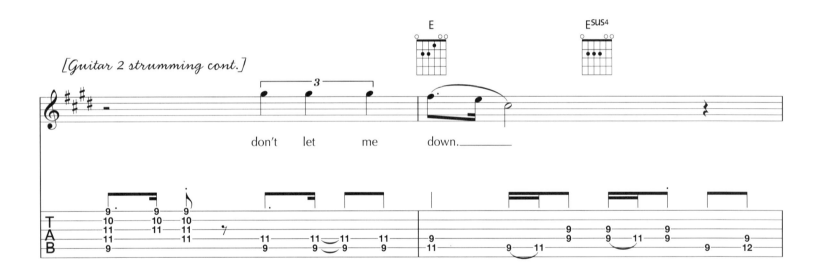
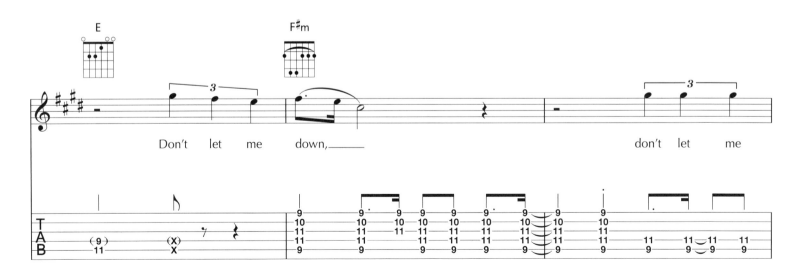

Dear Prudence

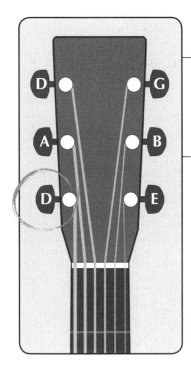

Inspired by Prudence Farrow, who accompanied the Beatles to India in 1968, 'Dear Prudence' was John's message of concern to their companion at her seeming unwillingness to relax and 'join in the fun'.

Tuning

The main guitar part is in drop D tuning: the 6th string is tuned to D. This tuning is ideal for the finger-picking style used, which mainly plays chords on the top three strings while the bottom three strings remain open for much of the time.

The Picking Pattern

The finger-picking used in this song is based around an alternating bass note pattern popularised by Merle Travis' Country & Western style, known as *Travis Picking*. The basic pattern is played with the thumb like so:

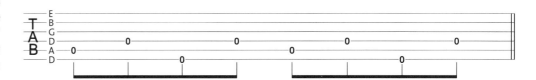

Notes are then added on top of this bass line in a syncopated pattern. Here's how it looks on a straightforward chord of D:

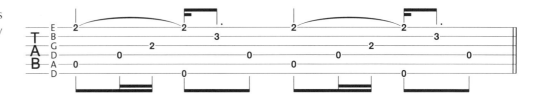

Watch the Video
Take a look at the video at 2:11 for a clear example of this picking pattern played on a high D6 shape.

Intro

The six-bar intro establishes the picking pattern and the final two bars—labelled as *guitar figure 1*—are played at various points throughout the song.

The chord shapes begin up on the 14th fret, gradually descending all the way down the neck. By the final two bars, the descending line is transferred to the bass.

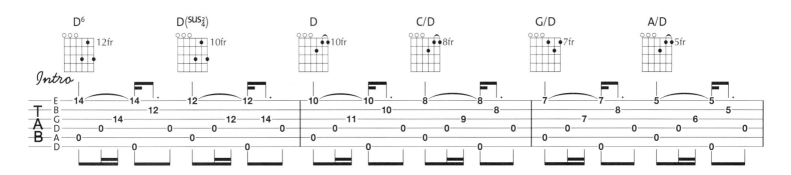

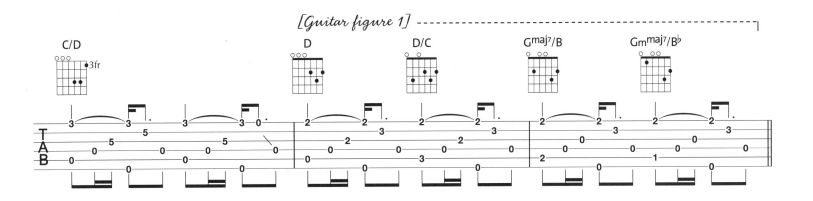

Verse 1

🎞 02:58

The guitar part for the verse simply plays *guitar figure 1* seven times with a variation on the sixth time, where the second bar moves to chords of C and G.

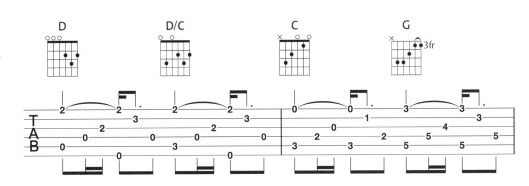

Verse 2

🎞 03:32

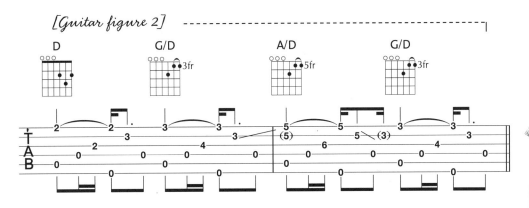

The second verse is just like the first, but with a different ending: a sequence of four shapes on the top three strings, labelled as *guitar figure 2*.

Moving Chord Shape

Simply keep the shape from the end of verse 2 and reposition it at the frets shown in the tab.

Bridge

🎞 03:48

In this section, *guitar figure 2* is played twice through, before the same three-string shape is played on the 1st fret, 4th fret and 3rd fret (*right*):

Watch out for the 2/4 bar: just count two beats instead of the usual four.

The bridge finishes off with a single play through of *guitar figure 1*.

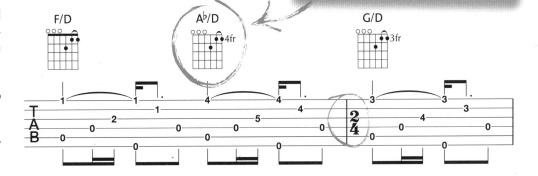

33

Bridge: Lead Guitar

`04:29`

While the main guitar part picks as usual, a lead guitar plays a single note line. It's a two-bar phrase with various hammer-ons and bends:

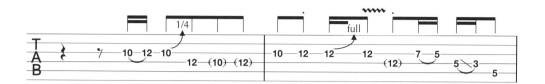

This phrase is repeated, and then at the end of the 2/4 bar there's a slide down the 6th string to a sustained open note.

It's probably easiest to watch the video to see exactly how this is done.

Verses 3 & 4

`05:03`

Lead Guitar Line

Look at the song tab to see the full lead guitar line for verse 3.

The lead line that begins in the bridge continues into verse 3 in an ad lib. series of phrases, culminating eventually in a single strummed chord of D at the end of the verse.

At this point the main guitar part, that up till now had been picking the familiar *guitar figure 1* chords, switches to strumming the same shapes in eighths and sixteenths (*below*):

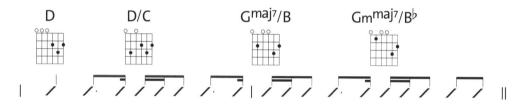

This strumming continues into verse 4 for 8 bars before changing to steady eighths for a further four bars.

The lead guitar, meanwhile, plays further improvised lines, eventually rising to the 22nd fret.

Finally, with the lead guitar playing a high trilled note, the main guitar picks the variant we saw in verse 1, ending on a bar of D (*right*):

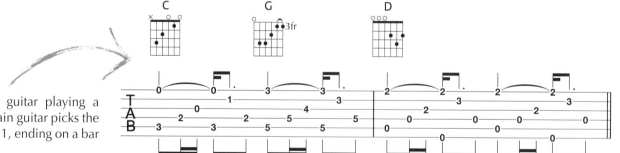

Outro

`07:51`

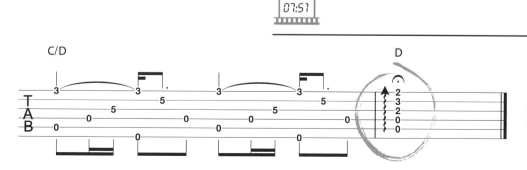

The final section is identical to the first four bars of the intro, but finishing on a held, strummed, chord of D.

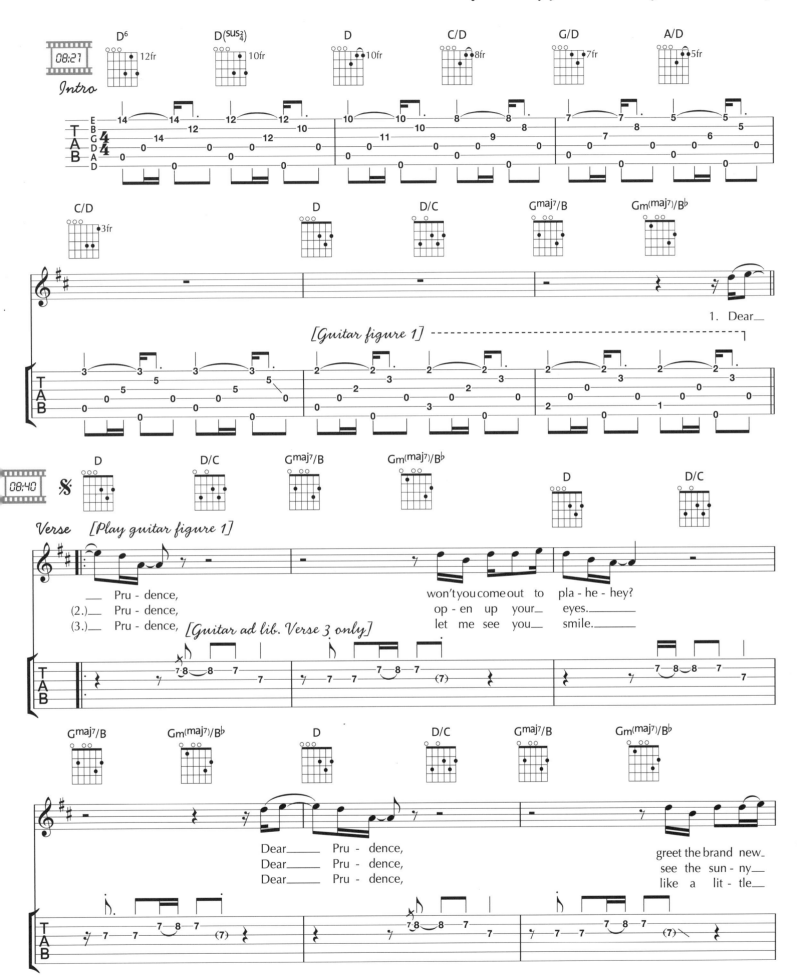

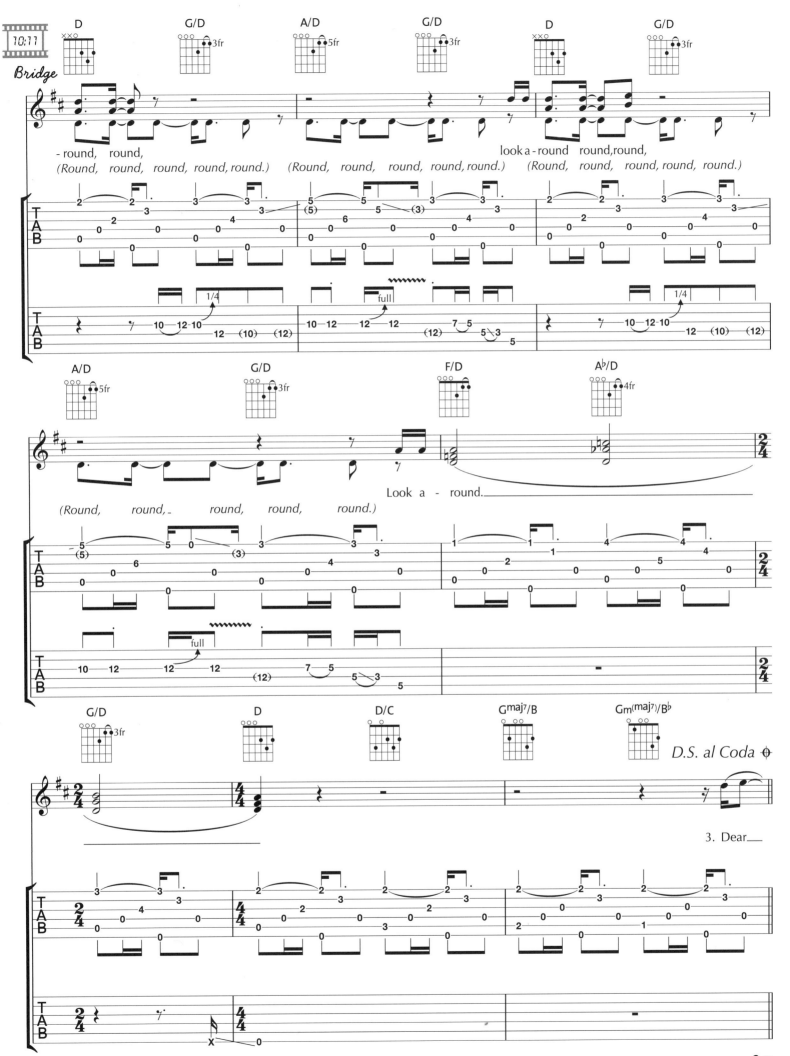

Get Back

Originally heard as a single in 1969, the version released in the US was the Beatles' first song to be recorded in full stereo. The guitar plays a prominent part throughout with riffs, licks and strumming, too.

Palm Muting

Rest the heel of the palm at or very near the bridge and just touching the strings. This will shorten the sustain of the strings, creating a muted effect. This way, the individual notes can be heard very clearly as they don't blend together.

Intro

Play the bottom two strings in even eighths, strumming down every time. Accent the strums on the beat, but mute them slightly with the palm.

The off-beat notes are played a little softer but aren't muted. Watch the video to hear how this sounds. It should create a steady chugging texture.

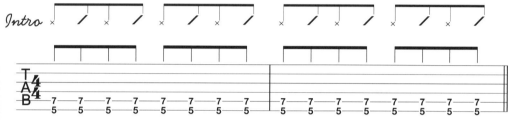

Verse 1

In the verse, the intro rhythm develops into a riff very like the one we saw in 'Back in the U.S.S.R.' (page 11).

Strummed down in eighths as before, the mini-chord has a fifth-string note that alternates to a note two frets higher.

Here it is on the 5th fret for A, which is played for two bars at the start of the verse:

Now it slides up to the 10th fret for a D chord for a bar:

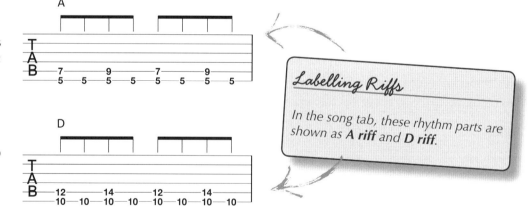

Labelling Riffs

In the song tab, these rhythm parts are shown as **A riff** and **D riff**.

The rhythm then breaks for a bar, playing instead this fill with slides and half-step bends:

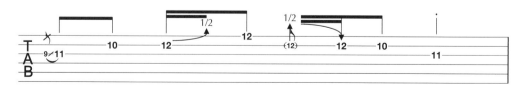

For verse 1, these four bars just repeat. Named *A riff* and *D riff* in the song tab, these labels reappear in various other sections of the song as indicated to save space. As we'll see, verse 2 is almost identical.

40

Chorus 1

`02:35`

The chorus has the exact same form as the verse, and you can play the *A strum* and *D strum* rhythm parts as before. A second guitar plays new riffs, however. Firstly, on a chord of A, a single-note line is followed by sixteenth strumming on the top strings:

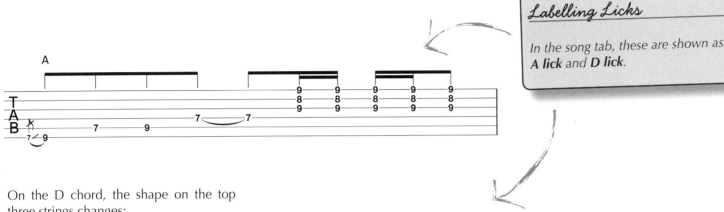

> **Labelling Licks**
>
> In the song tab, these are shown as **A lick** and **D lick**.

On the D chord, the shape on the top three strings changes:

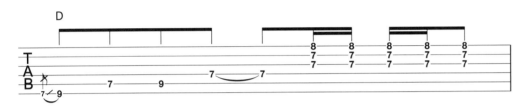

Chorus 2

`03:44`

The second chorus is strummed just like the verse, with the *A riff* and *D riff* patterns.

At the end of the chorus, however, the A strum is played for three bars, sliding up to a pair of notes on the 4th and 5th strings. Here are the last three bars:

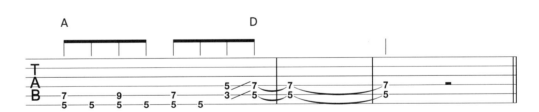

Piano Solo

`04:11`

Following the second chorus, the piano solo is accompanied by a combination of the elements we've already seen: two bars of the *A riff*, one of the *D riff*, and then the *A lick* from the chorus.

The form is the same as the verse, so these four bars repeat to make eight bars in all.

> **Learning the Form**
>
> Take a good look at all the sections of the song to see how they fit together. And try memorising complete sections: you'll find you can concentrate much more on playing the music.

Verse 2 Ending

In the song tab, verse 2 is played at the segno (𝄋) and the different ending is clearly indicated.

Verse 2

The second verse is identical to the first, but with a different fill in the final bar:

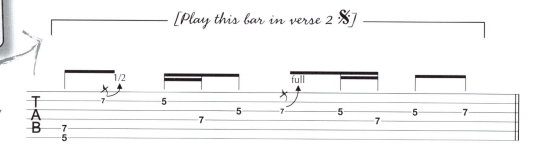

Final Chorus

The third chorus, which follows the second guitar solo, again ends with a held D chord. This time, it rings on for three full bars and another bar of two beats:

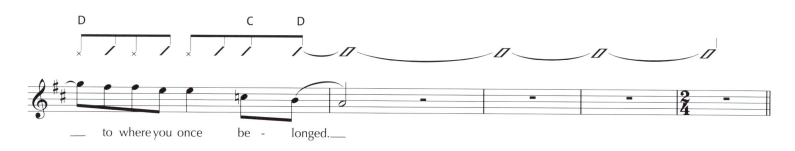

Guitar Solos

Be sure to check out the video, which gives a complete rendition of the two guitar solos. They're also fully notated in the song tab.

Outro

The song ends on a combination of elements from the verse and chorus, just like in the piano solo. The fade out is a repeat of the *A lick* and *D lick*:

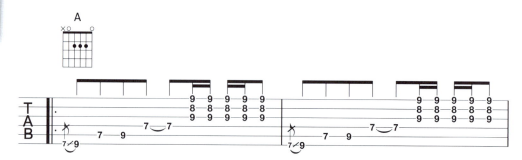

Repeat ad lib. to fade

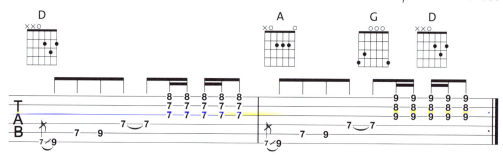

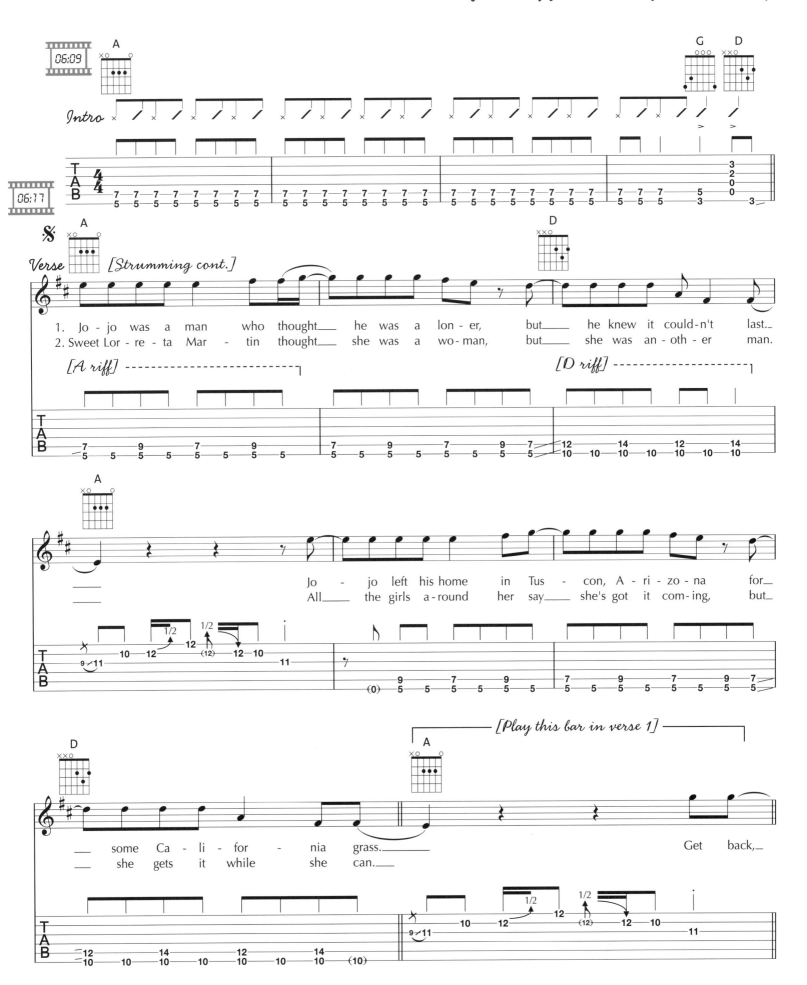

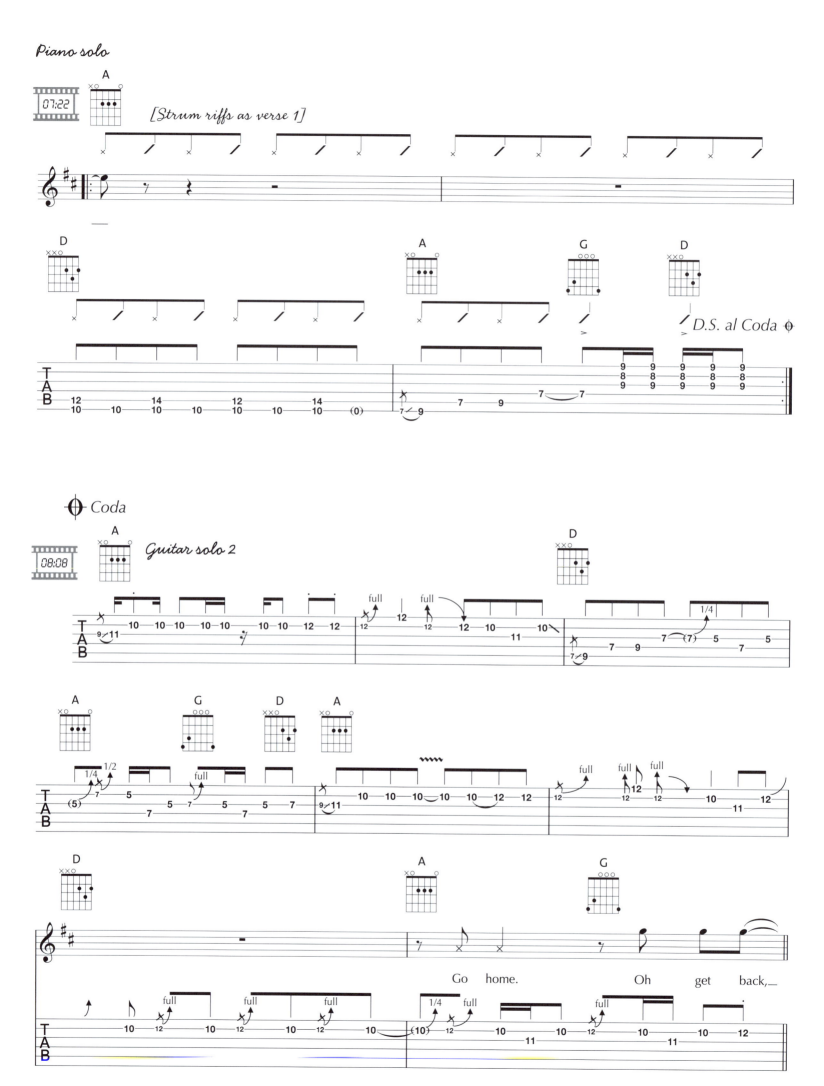

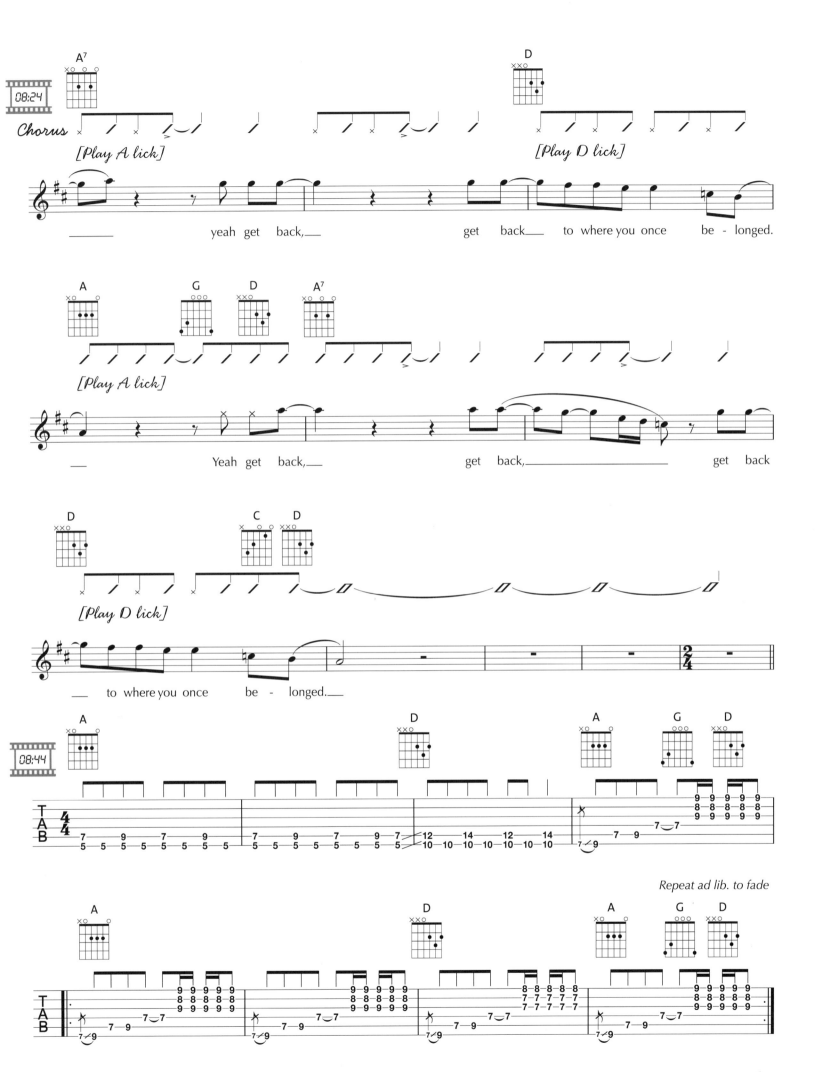

Lucy In The Sky With Diamonds

This Sgt. Pepper's *classic was recorded at Abbey Road studios in early March, 1967. The changes of time signature and tempo create a surreal daydream of shifting moods and hallucinations.*

Playing the Intro

You can play either the keyboard part arranged for guitar, or else strum through the chords in straight quarter-notes.

The chord shapes are played on the bottom four strings to provide contrast to the lead line. Here are both together:

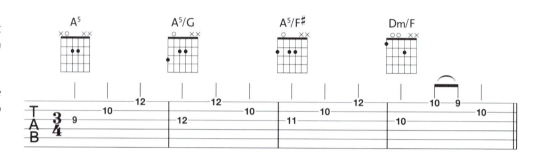

Verse Variations

This lead line is played another four times in the verse, with variations.

On the second time through we have this five-bar version, ending on two bars of F:

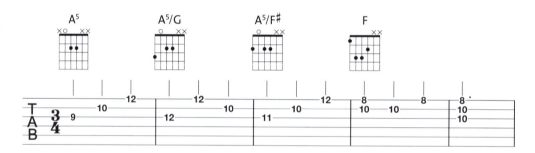

On the fourth time through there's a six-bar variation ending on Dm with a changing bass line:

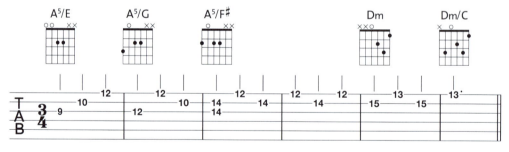

Pre-Chorus

Strum through the chords in steady quarter-notes, or else play the lead guitar line with bends that echoes the vocal melody.

Here are the final few bars. Notice the change in time signature. It's now in a solid—and slower—four quarter-note beats to the bar.

> **Tempo Change**
>
> At the end of the pre-chorus, the quarter-note tempo slows as the time signature changes to four-in-the-bar.

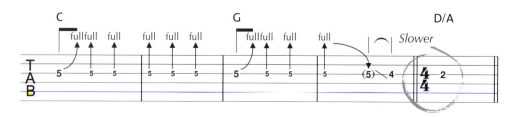

48

Chorus

Again you can strum the chord shapes shown in steady quarter-notes, or play the single-note guitar line.

It's a two-bar phrase played three times with variations—and an extra bar added at the end.

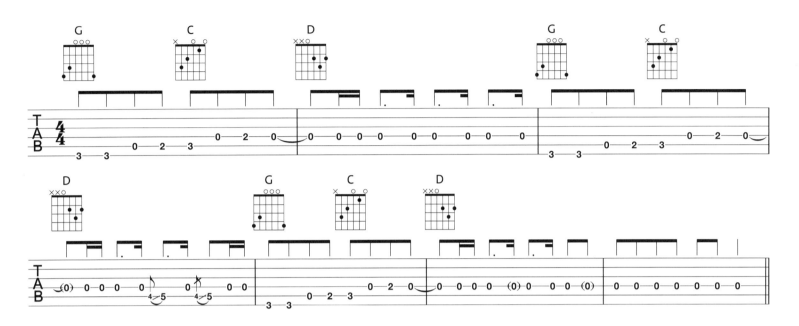

Other Details

There are slight differences between verses 1 and 2. In the song tab these are shown by an *ossia* staff floating above the main guitar part. This *ossia* is also used to show the variation between the first and second pre-chorus.

Ossia

Slight differences or optional parts are shown in a separate ossia staff to save rewriting an entire section.

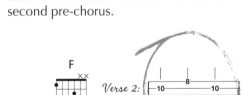

Outro

The outro is an 8-bar variation on the chorus, repeating to a fade. Play the first two bars of the chorus three times (6 bars), and then the new two-bar part shown. It's a rhythm on the 4th string switching to the 5th fret of the bottom string and ending on a slide down. Here's the original two-bar phrase followed by the new part:

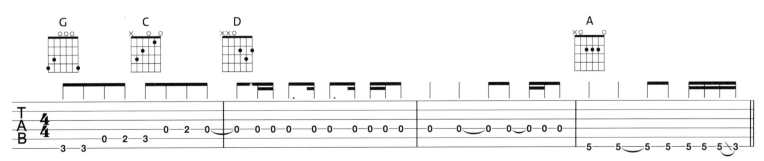

49

Sgt. Pepper's Lonely Hearts Club Band

The title track from The Beatles' influential 1967 concept album opens the record and reappears as a reprise towards the end. The song features three separate guitar parts, including one in drop D tuning.

Intro

[Gtr 1] `01:29` — The electric lead line that opens the song contains a single note that requires drop D tuning (see page 32). Play it with a fuzzy distortion:

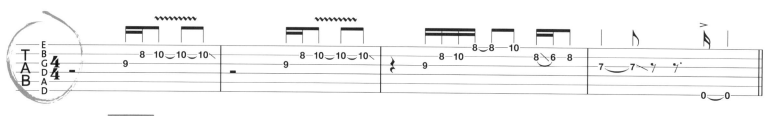

[Gtr 2] `01:51` — The 2nd guitar, in standard tuning, meanwhile plays this rhythmic riff with a crunchy distortion effect:

[Gtr 3] `02:09` — The rhythm guitar strums constantly on the bottom two or three strings. Again this guitar has distortion added that creates a very heavy, grungy sound.

Verse 1

[Gtr 1] `02:30` — In the 8-bar verse, the 1st guitar plays off-beat chords on the top four strings only, emphasised and detached. It ends with a lick in the last two bars:

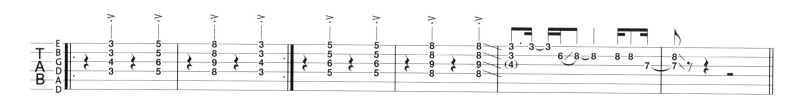

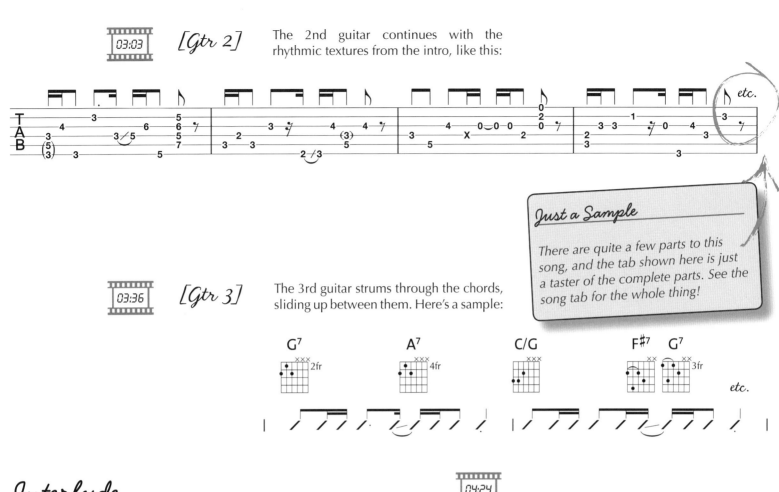

Interlude

On the original recording, a French horn section now takes over. Either strum through in simple eighths, or play the horn line:

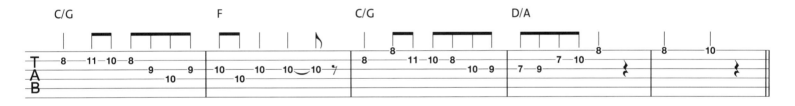

Chorus

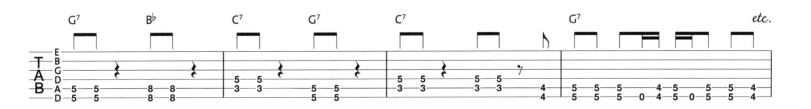

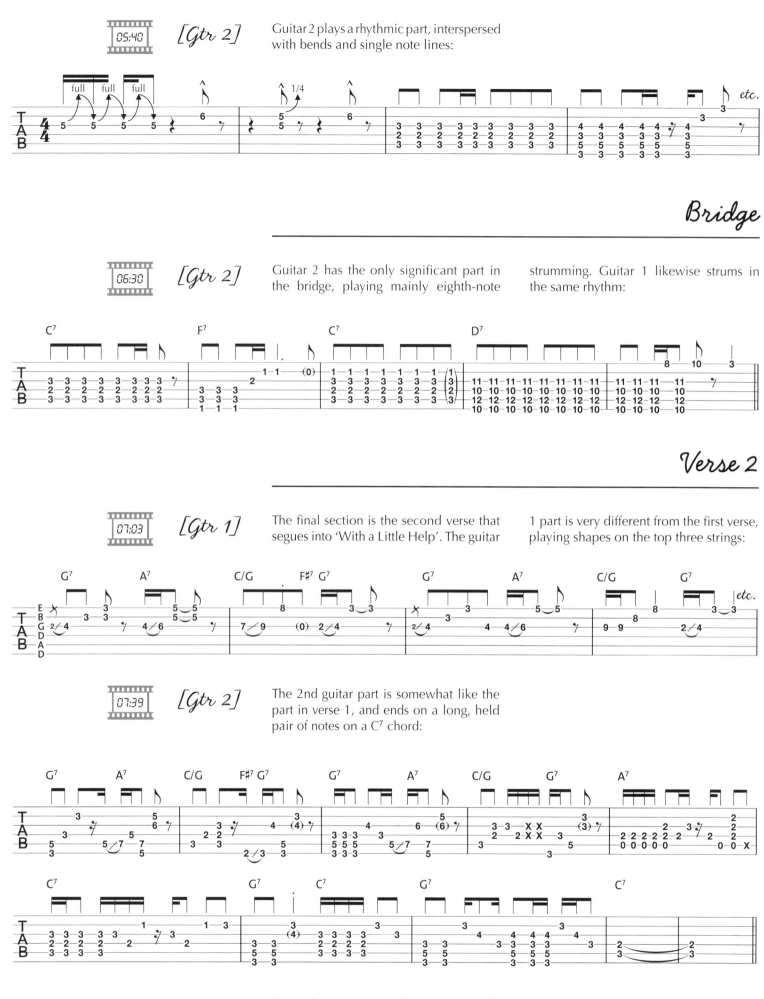

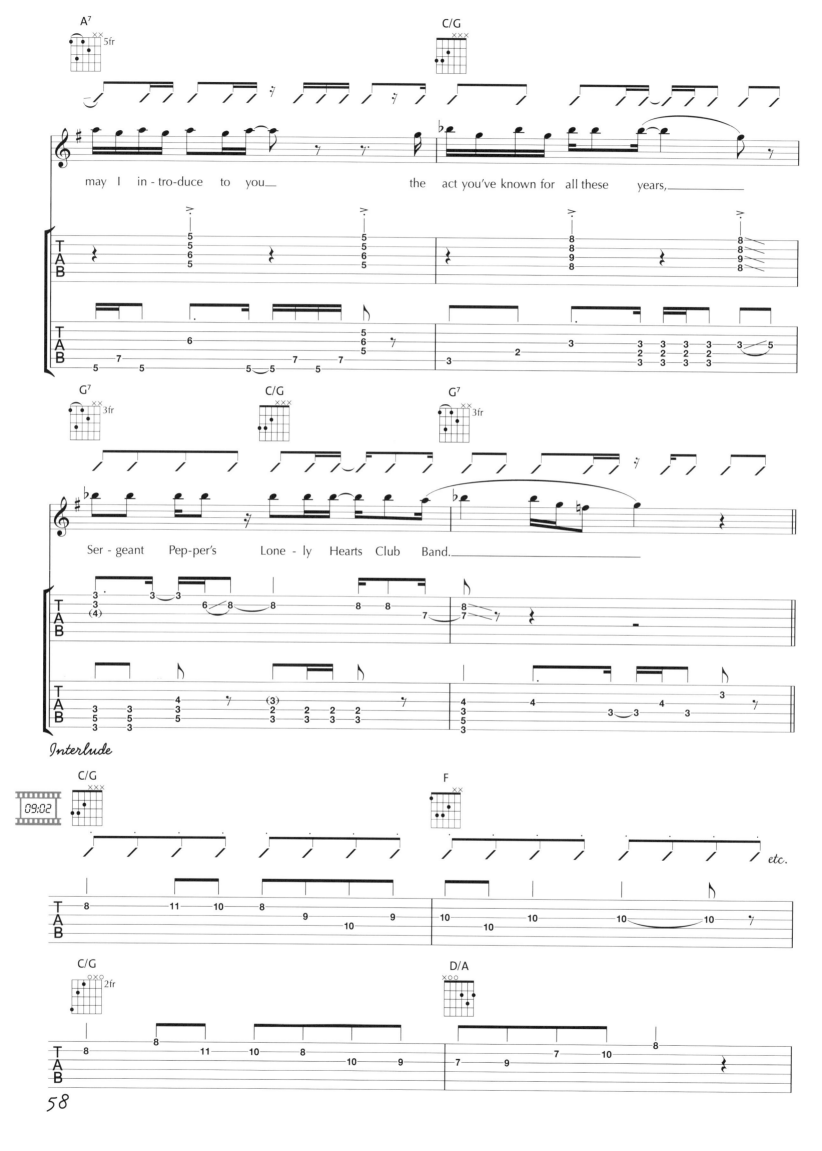

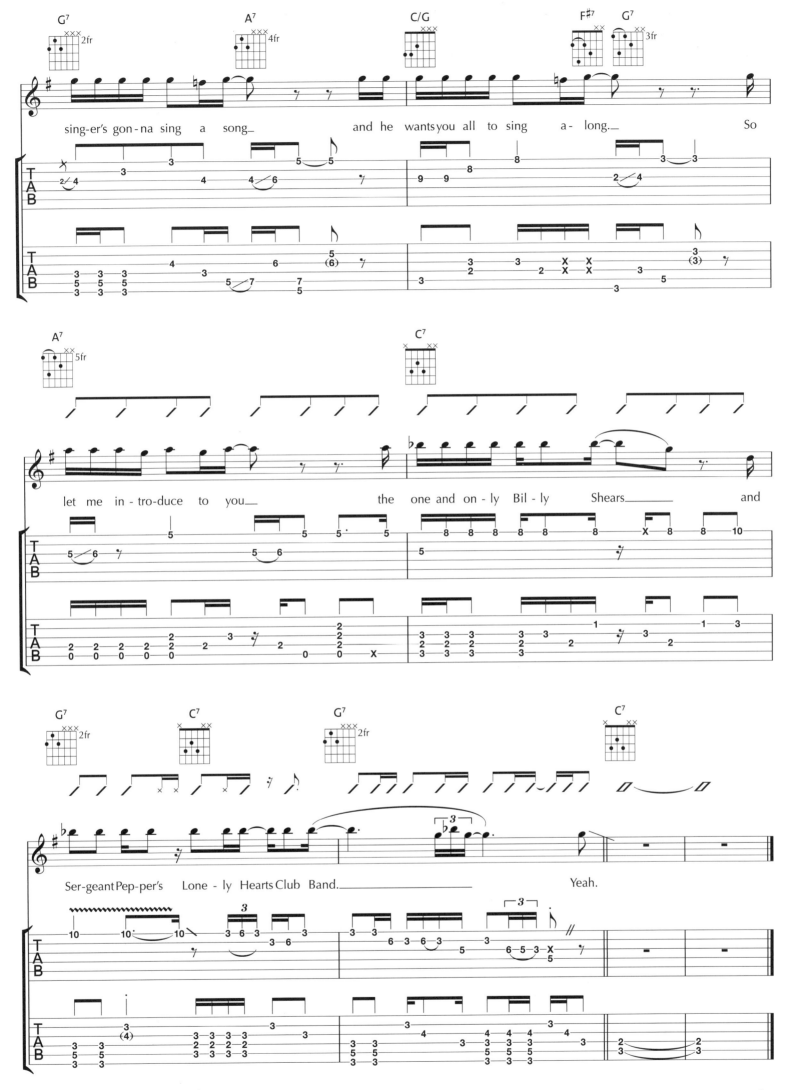

Reading Tablature

Guitar tablature—or 'tab'—is a system of notation based on a set of six lines, each representing a string of the guitar.

The music is divided into sections of equal length called *bars* or *measures* shown with bar lines.

Fret Numbers

The numbers relate to frets. Play the note on the string indicated at the fret number shown. Here, play a note at the 7th fret of the 2nd string.

Bar Lines

Vertical lines divide the music into short measures or bars. Longer sections are divided up with double bar lines.

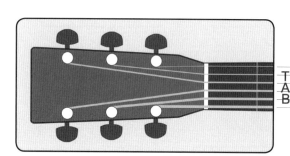

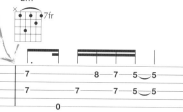

Stacked Notes

Notes shown one above the other are played at the same time.

The *time signature* at the start of the music will tell you how many beats each bar has.

The top number gives the beat count, while the bottom number indicates what kind of note value is used to show the beat.

In this example (*right*) the music has four beats in the bar, and the note value used for one beat is a quarter-note. Quarter-notes are by far the commonest type of beat and are almost universally used in rock and pop music.

How many beats?

What type?

$\frac{4}{4}$

Time Signature Changes

Occasionally, a bar with a different number of beats appears. This is shown by a new, temporary time signature.

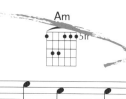
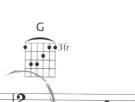

Pla - net Earth_ is blue and there's no-thing I can do.
Pla - net Earth_ is blue and there's no-thing I can do.

62

Reading Rhythms

Apart from the standard music notation used for the vocal line, both the strumming patterns and guitar tab have rhythm tails: a special notation that makes it easy to see how long a note lasts—and when no note is played, too.

Let's look at the way rhythms are shown in strumming patterns.

Firstly, a **whole note**, lasting a bar of 4/4. An absence of notes is called a *rest*. In the UK, whole notes are known as *semibreves*.

A **half-note**, or *minim*, lasts half as long as a whole note. In 4/4 it's worth two beats. Here's a bar each of half-notes and half-note rests.

A **quarter-note**, or *crotchet*, is worth a quarter of a whole-note. It represents a single beat in 4/4.

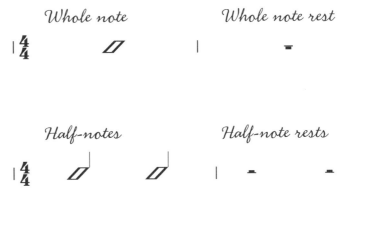

Dividing quarter-notes in half creates **eighth-notes**. These can appear singly—with a hook on the stem; or else in pairs—with a beam joining them. Eighth-note rests are also shown.

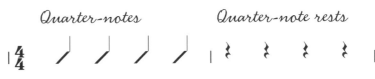

The smallest commonly-used rhythm value is the **sixteenth-note**, or *semiquaver*. These appear singly or in groups of up to four together (a single beat).

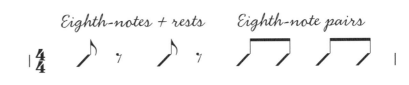

Adding a dot after any note creates a time value of half as much again. A **dotted quarter**, for instance, is worth three eighths. A **dotted half** is worth three quarters. Notice that dotted eighths are paired with single sixteenths to make a whole beat.

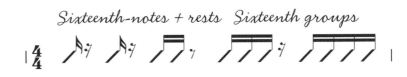

Notes are joined together to create unusual time values or to continue across a bar line. Curved lines called **ties** are used to connect notes into a single note.

Reading Rhythms in Tablature

You'll find guitar tablature *with* rhythm tails, and other tablature *without* (often used together with standard guitar notation). This book uses tab with rhythm tails, to give you more precise information. The tails follow almost precisely the same rules as for strumming rhythms, with one exception which we'll look at now.

Here's a strumming pattern with the equivalent in guitar tab below. The rhythm tails and rests are exactly the same.

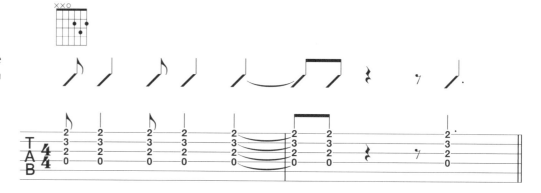

In tablature, half-notes have a rhythm tail which is identical to a quarter-note.

However, it's almost always easy to tell half-notes from quarter-notes by their position in the bar and/or other notes and rests around it.

A whole note, of course, has no tail at all.

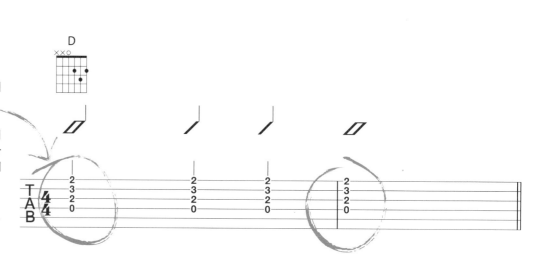

Guitar Instructions

The arrangements in this book include full tablature for the guitar part of every riff, strumming or picking part you'll need.

Where the same part reappears later in the song, it's generally indicated in square brackets (*right*).

So look out for these instructions: they'll refer to a part already played, or else a detail covered in the tutorial section.

[Picking as chorus]

Guitar Instructions

Watch out for these labels in the music. They'll show you what to play for any part that's already previously appeared in tablature.